J
597
OHA

O'Hare, Ted

Fish

DEMCO

Fish

WHAT IS AN ANIMAL?

Ted O'Hare

Rourke

Publishing LLC

Vero Beach, Florida 32964

www.rourkepublishing.com

PHOTO CREDITS: © Digital Vision, LTD: Cover photo; © Breck P. Kent: pages 12, 20; © Marty Snyderman: pages 5, 7, 8, 13, 15, 17; © Lynn M. Stone: title page, pages 11, 19

Title page: A sockeye salmon returns to the stream of its birth to spawn and die.

Editor: Frank Sloan

Cover and interior design by Nicola Stratford

Library of Congress Cataloging-in-Publication Data

O'Hare, Ted, 1961-
    Fish / Ted O'Hare.
        p. cm. -- (What is an animal?)
    Includes bibliographical references and index.
    ISBN 1-59515-417-5 (hardcover)
    1. Fishes--Juvenile literature. I. Title. II. Series: O'Hare, Ted,
1961-   What is an animal?
    QL617.2.O33 2006
    597--dc22

Printed in the USA

CG/CG

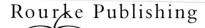

Rourke Publishing

www.rourkepublishing.com – sales@rourkepublishing.com
Post Office Box 3328, Vero Beach, FL 32964

1-800-394-7055

Table of Contents

Fish

Fish are **vertebrates**. This means they have backbones. Amphibians, reptiles, birds and mammals are vertebrates, too. Fish differ in many ways from the other groups.

Fish have fins, they live in water, and they usually have scales. Almost all **species** of fish breathe through **gills** instead of lungs.

Fish are **cold-blooded,** as are reptiles and amphibians. This means their body temperature is close to that of the water around them.

Shape, fins, and scales help identify fish.

Fish Habits

Most fish are active swimmers. They swim to find food, hiding places, and places to lay their eggs. Some fish make long journeys. Pacific salmon travel from the sea. They go back to lay eggs in the freshwater rivers where they were born. Other fish swim only short distances.

DID YOU KNOW?

Many fish species live in large groups known as **schools**. Others live by themselves.

A large school of snappers searches for food.

Kinds of Fish

Scientists have found about 22,000 species of fish. Most of them have skeletons of bone. Another group has skeletons of **cartilage**.

Cartilage bends, and it is lighter than bone. The frame of your nose is cartilage. Almost 1,800 kinds of fish, including sharks and rays, have skeletons of cartilage.

The bat ray has a skeleton mostly of cartilage.

Where Fish Live

Fish live wherever there is water. Most species live in the ocean. However, more than 8,000 species live in freshwater lakes and rivers.

Some fish live in a mixture of fresh water and salt water. And some travel back and forth between the two.

10

Red sockeye salmon return from the sea to freshwater streams like this to lay their eggs.

The pan-shaped flounder hides on the bottom of the sea.

An eel is shaped like a snake, but it is a fish.

Fish Bodies

A fish's body is shaped to help it survive. Tuna are fast-swimming fish. Their bodies have shapes like a torpedo. Fish that live on the ocean bottom are often flat.

Most fish bodies are smooth and streamlined. Their color matches their surroundings in the water. Some fish are brightly colored, while others are not.

A shark's torpedo shape helps it swim easily.

Amazing Fish

Fish are amazing for many reasons. At 40 feet (12 meters) long, the whale shark is very big. Yet it lives on tiny plants and animals known as **plankton**. The walking catfish moves over land by using its fins like feet. Some fish, deep in the ocean bottom, can make their own light!

DID YOU KNOW?

A few fish can even breathe air. And some can "fly" by skipping across the water's surface.

16

A diver swims with a whale shark, the world's largest fish.

Predator and Prey

Most fish are **predators**. Bluefish, piranhas, barracudas, and some kinds of sharks are predators. They catch other animals, or **prey**, for food. Fish are prey for snakes, eagles, pelicans, otters, and seals.

Predator fish usually eat other fish. Great white sharks, however, kill seals. A few fish eat clams and other little creatures with shells.

This brown bear has caught its salmon prey in Alaska.

Baby Fish

Most fish hatch from eggs. The female may lay her eggs in a "nest" in water.

Some fish eggs may hatch inside the mother. These fish bear their young alive. An example of this is the great white shark.

DID YOU KNOW?

Baby fish are known as **fry**. They may look much like their parents, or they may not. It depends upon the species.

A newly hatched rainbow trout will live on egg yolk for a short time.

21

People and Fish

Fish are important to people for food and sport. Fishing boats catch millions of pounds of fish. Many kinds of fish are raised on fish farms.

Fish help preserve the balance of nature. Healthy rivers, lakes, and oceans are needed to keep fish alive. Many species of fish, however, have become scarce because of pollution and too much fishing.

GLOSSARY

cartilage (KART ul ij) — the strong, flexible body tissue that makes up most of a shark's or ray's skeleton

cold-blooded (KOLD BLUD ed) — refers to animals whose body temperatures stay about the same as those of their surroundings; fish, amphibians, and reptiles are cold-blooded

fry (FRY) — small, young fish

gills (GILZ) — organs that help fish and certain other animals breathe by taking oxygen from water

plankton (PLANGK tun) — tiny floating plants and animals of the sea and other bodies of water

predators (PRED uh terz) — animals that hunt other animals for food

prey (PRAY) — an animal that is hunted by other animals for food

schools (SKOOLZ) — groups of fish that swim together

species (SPEE sheez) — within a group of closely related animals, one certain kind, such as a rainbow trout

vertebrates (VER tuh BRAYTZ) — animals with backbones; fish, amphibians, reptiles, birds, and mammals are vertebrates

Index

Further Reading

Arlon, Penelope. *DK First Animal Encyclopedia*. Dorling Kindersley, 2004

Pascoe, Elaine. *Animals with Backbones*. Powerkids Press, 2003

Solway, Andrew. *Classifying Fish*. Heinemann Library, 2003

Websites to Visit

http://www.biologybrowser.org

http://www.kidport.com/RefLib/Science/Animals/AnimalIndexV.htm

http://www.fisheries.nsw.gov.au/kids/

About the Author

Ted O'Hare is an author and editor of children's books. He divides his time between New York City and a home upstate.